Whittling the Old Time Way

by

JACK D. JACKSON

FIRST EDITION   Copyright © 2009 by Jack D. Jackson
Published in the United States of America by Eakin Press, a division of Sunbelt Media,
Inc., P.O. Box 21235   Waco, Texas 76702
email: sales@eakinpress.com   website: www.eakinpress.com
ALL RIGHTS RESERVED.
1   2   3   4   5   6   7   8   9
ISBN 13: 978-1-934645-45-1
ISBN 10: 1-934645-45-1
Library of Congress Control Number 2009932550

Contents

Dedicated to my wife, Sue, of course

    In the introduction to Book 1, *How to Whittle the Whimsies of Yesterday*, I said we had half a handful of grandkids. Now, two years later, how blessed we are. In a few short months there will be a WHOLE handful, with names starting with the first letter of the alphabet to the last letter in the alphabet. We literally have grandchildren from A to Z.

Introduction

When I started thinking about Book 2, I pondered and re-thought how I had gone into so much detail in illustrating things like the Wooden Chain and Slider in Book 1.

I wanted Book 2 to have more complicated projects, but at the same time be a smaller book that I could sell for less.

With these things in mind, it became apparent. To go into such great detail in Book 2 would be a redundancy and therefore boring.

The wooden chain, in my opinion, will always be the foundation for the whimsie whittler.

Doing projects in Book 2 like the Love Spoons Joined by the Wooden Chain would take up the whole book if I went into the same great detail as I did in Book 1.

So, upon final thought I decided to omit a lot of photos and writing, and dwell more on setting the guidelines for these new projects.

Then, if for some reason you have a problem, you can always refer to Book 1, which I hope you already have.

The tools used in Book 2 are basically the same as in Book 1, with a couple of exceptions.

Doing things is the only way I learn—by trial and error, so to speak.

On a good whittling day I spend some eight to ten hours. I was working on a small Ball in a Cage, when the knife nicked the cage bar, and like a bolt of lightning the thought hit me …

I took a knife I seldom use and went to my shop where I do my sharpening and grinding. By grinding away the sharp edge of the knife and leaving the round point, in about ten minutes I had invented Knife #1 in photo of Knives Used in Book 2 that would not cut the bars of the cage.

So it goes. Necessity is the mother of invention.

Another simple thing I use since I wrote Book 1 is a spiral scroll saw blade.

Take a spiral scroll saw blade and cut it in half. Epoxy the two pieces in a wooden handle.

Make the teeth on one blade point toward the handle, the other away from the handle. This makes a very, very small rasp which I use to clean the inside of the small chain links shown in Tools for Special Grooves.

From time to time I will put new ideas on my web site that will be helpful to my whittling friends around the world.

May the good Lord bless.

—JACK JACKSON
www.howtowhittle.com

Foreword

In memory of our fathers, grandfathers and all those great pioneers who made this the greatest nation the world has ever known.

Since the dawn of time, man has learned to survive by trial and error. And the foremost tool in surviving dates back through the ages—the knife.

The first knives were simple shards of flint, broken perhaps by hammering two rocks together and picking the one with the sharpest edge. They were used to cut, scrape, and do the things for their basic survival.

Knives were an evolution over thousands of years, and only in the last few centuries has the knife as we know it come into being.

The first steel-bladed knives were not folding pocket knives, but knives like the Bowie knife, the kind the famous mountain men carried, like Kit Carson, Jim Bridger and the thousands of others who tamed the Wild West.

In the late 1800s, a folding pocket knife was one of man's most prized possessions, second only to his wife, gun and dog.

A knife with a small, medium, and large blade that could be carried in your pocket was a revolution that started chips flying around the country.

Tools for Special Grooves

Left to right, #1, ⅛-wide No. 3 gouge; #2, ³/₁₆ No. 5 gouge; #3, homemade ³/₁₆-inch screwdriver knife; #4, homemade ⅛-inch screwdriver knife. Screwdriver knives are used to make straight-in cuts; #5, small hand drill; #6, two spiral scroll saw blades epoxyed in a wooden handle (makes a good, very small rasp for inside small chain links); #7, dental pick; #8, small hobby saw with a #15 keyhole saw blade.

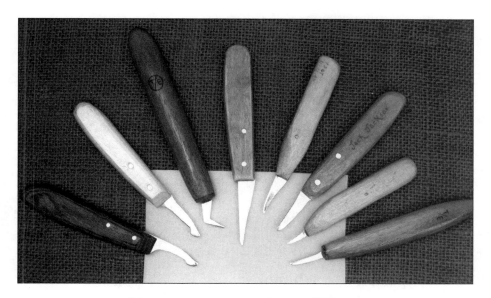

Knives Used in Book 2

Left to right, #1, ball-whittling knife (takes the place of old round, pointed knife used in Book 1); #2, smaller ball-whittling knife; #3, hook-bill knife (used to make undercuts, like around the spindle of Ball in a Ball that Turns in a Cage); #4, long, thin blade; #5, smaller thin blade; #6, good whittling blade $1\frac{1}{4}$-inch long; #7, small blade $\frac{1}{2}$-inch long; #8, small, round, pointed blade $\frac{7}{8}$-inch long.

Doughnut on a Pencil

Our projects in Book 1 started with sharpening a stick to look like a pencil, so we'll take the pencil a step further.

Let's use a 1-inch square piece of bass wood 10 inches long. Sharpen it to look like the pencil in Book 1.

Then add a doughnut. Yes, I said a doughnut. Do you think I'm a bit nutty? Doughnuts and pencils don't go together, you say.

Well, we will just start us a new trend.

When you get the pencil to a point, like shown here, start rounding the square stick.

Round for the entire length, this will be some real good whittling.

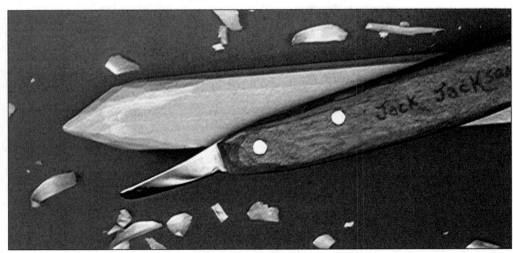

Photo #2

When all the really good whittling is done, and the stick is round, measure 3 inches from the end and draw a line around the pencil.

Then draw a second line ⅜-inch from the first line. This will be the doughnut.

Now, as shown in Photo #4, make a straight-in cut on both lines about 3/16-inch deep.

These cuts will have to be deepened as we whittle away the unwanted wood.

Be very careful with straight-in cuts on round wood, it can roll and cause a bad cut.

Photo #3

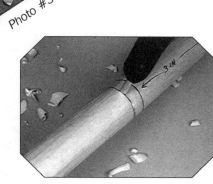

Photo #4

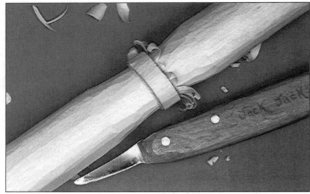

Photo #5

In Photo #5, starting 1¼ inch each side of the doughnut, I have whittled down to the depth of the straight-in cut.

Now deepen the straight-in cut again repeating the whittling and straight-in cuts until the stick for the doughnut is about ½ inch in diameter (Photo #6).

With the small blade knife, slice in ⅛-inch deep on both sides as in Photo #7. In Photo #8, I use a small ⅛ #3 gouge to pry out chips by digging in at an angle.

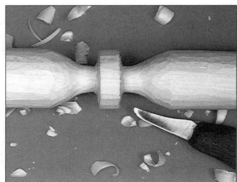

Photo #6

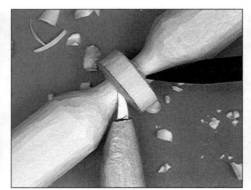

Photo #7

Photo #8

When you have both sides gouged out about ⅛-inch deep, you should be able to work a thin knife blade or a saw blade through the remainder of the wood left between the pencil and the doughnut (Photo #9).

When the doughnut is free, the pencil can be cleaned up with a small blade knife. (Photo #10)

Then round off the edges of the doughnut and this part of the pencil with a doughnut is done (Photo #11).

This could very well be the only doughnut on a pencil in the whole wide world; however, let's go a step further and put the finishing touches on our masterpiece.

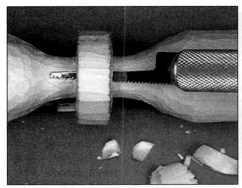

Photo #9

Photo #10

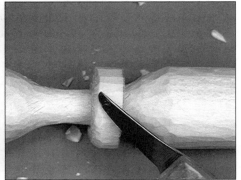

Photo #11

After all, most pencils are a bright yellow and have an eraser, some lead and the name of the company who made it and where.

In this case, the company who made it was you, and you can be sure it will be a great conversation piece when you just happen to leave it out on your desk.

A friend may say, "This thing won't write." You can say, "Yeah, but it has a doughnut in case you need a little snack!."

Photo #12

Heart in a Heart

The Heart in a Heart is one of my favorite pieces.

It is done here in a ¾-inch thick piece of bass wood. It is shown here in actual size so you can trace it onto your block of wood.

Draw the little heart on both sides of the big heart.

Now let's round off the edges to make it a little easier to hold.

When it's finished, the little heart will be free to move around inside the big heart.

Photo #1

Photo #2

After you have the little heart drawn and centered on the big heart, the next step is to make a straight-in cut ⅛-inch deep on the little heart as shown in Photo #2.

Photo #4

Photo #3

The objective now is to start at the center of the little heart and shave toward the straight-in cut, rounding the little heart down to the straight-in cut.

When this step is done, the little heart should be as high in the center as it was originally. As shown in Photo #4, the slope of the little heart will now continue under the straight-in cut of the big heart as shown here in Photo #5. This will have to be done all the way around the little heart, until the cuts on both sides come together, giving the little heart room to move inside the big heart.

Photo #6

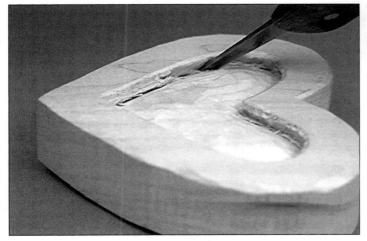

Photo #5

In Photo #6, the little heart is free to move; it is approximately the size of the pencil drawing on the big heart.

To make the heart look better, we can now whittle the edges of the big heart to a sloping bevel, starting near the pencil line and whittle

Photo #7   *Photo #8*

the edges of both sides of the big heart so as to look like the photos above. These photos are the same heart, just taken from different angles.

A heart in a heart like this one with a four-foot chain, all from one piece of wood, gets a blue ribbon at most shows I attend. See back of book.

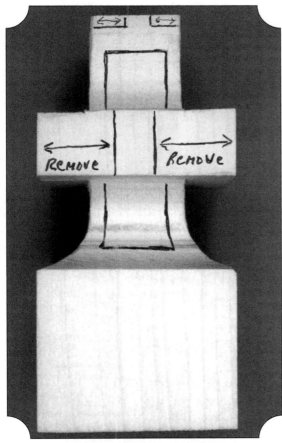

Photo #1 (actual size)

The Cross in a Cage

You will need a 2 x 2 block of bass wood 4¼ inches long, shown here in actual size so you can trace this pattern on your block of wood.

Saw to this shape and draw in the lines on all four sides.

The next step will be to remove the portions of wood where the arrows are, where the tiny arrows are on top, also.

A look at Photos #2 and #3 will help you visualize where we are going.

The cross is a step up from the simple Ball in a Cage, which most whittlers have already accomplished.

In Book 1, we did two balls in a cage.

The cross will have four sides that protrude out through the bars of the cage.

I have whittled away the wood (where the little arrow points) in Photo #2.

This will become the post for the cross, which the dotted lines simulate.

I have also whittled away and shaped one side to show how all four sides will look before we start to work to free the cross in its cage.

In Photo #3, I have shaped all four sides and completed the straight-in cuts, also removing some of the wood.

The cage bars can now be seen.

Photo #2

Photo #3

From Photo #3 to Photo #4 will take some whittling skill.

When you get to this point, the cross will be free from all four bars, but still attached at the top and bottom.

Photo #4

The bars of the cage curve out at the bottom and makes them very fragile. For this reason, I make the cut on the top first.

Photo #5

Simply work a thin knife blade around the post of the cross as shown here in Photo #5.

This is the same kind of cut we made to free the doughnut on the pencil.

When you have the post on top free, you can very carefully start whittling under the bottom of the post.

Whittling gently will take a bit longer, but it is better than rushing and breaking your master-piece.

The finished cross

Years ago, I bought a box of odds and ends. This piece of wood with a knot (Photo #6) was in the box. I modeled the finished cross in Photo #7 from the one with the knot, which has been a good conversation piece for a long time.

Photo #6

Photo #7

Two Ugly Faces

I use a 1½-inch square block of bass wood, 6 inches long, the extra length is safer to hold while carving your ugly face. We can later saw the bust to be about 3 inches tall.

The face on the left in Photo #1 is a long, happy face, which is 1⅝ inches down to the bottom of the nose and 2½ inches to the chin. The face on the right is ¼ inch shorter to the nose and chin, with a mouth that turns down to give him a frown.

In Photo #2, the finished happy face sits beside the face we will be doing. Start by rounding

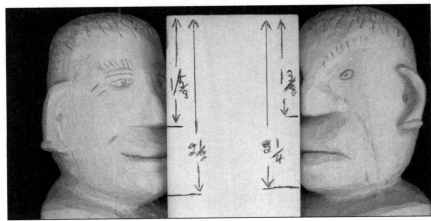

Photo #1

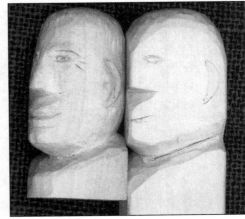

Photo #2

off the head and make a ³/₁₆-inch deep cut under the nose and a ½-inch deep cut under the chin, sloping up at the angle you can see in Photo #2 and #3.

To make the faces look completely different, we will curve the mouth slightly down as in Photo #3 and draw a line around the eyes and sloping down to the cut of the neck as shown in Photo #3 and the sketch drawn on the block in Photo #4.

The sketch is drawn on a block to give you an idea as to how to draw the lines on your block.

With the lines drawn, carve them out about ⅛-inch deep, taking a look at the finished face as you whittle.

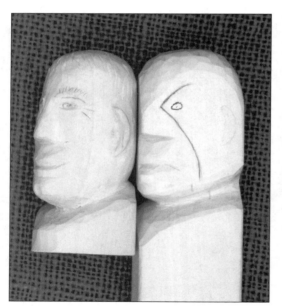

Photo #3

Photo #4

With the lines carved out ⅛-inch deep here in Photo #5, you can see how much difference it makes to carve out the deep wrinkle.

The two faces would look very much alike without this little change.

In Photo #6, the wood has been carved away around one ear, and starting on the other one.

The ear on a face is usually level with the eye on top and the upper lip on the bottom as the dotted lines show in Photo #5.

Photo #7, hollow out the shaded area on the unfinished ear.

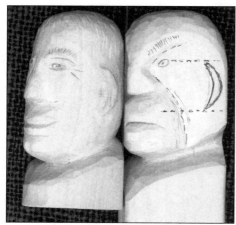

Photo #5

Photo #6

Photo #7

Two Ugly Faces

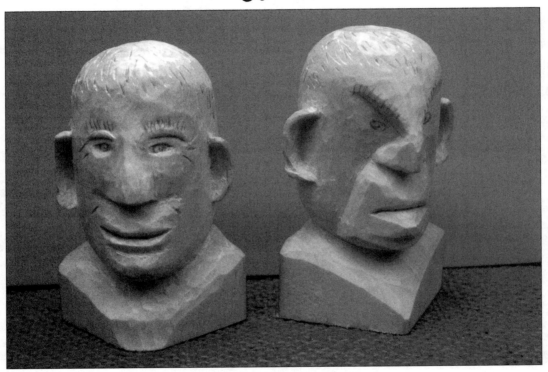

Chief Big Ear and his brother Buzzard Beak

Arrow Through the Heart

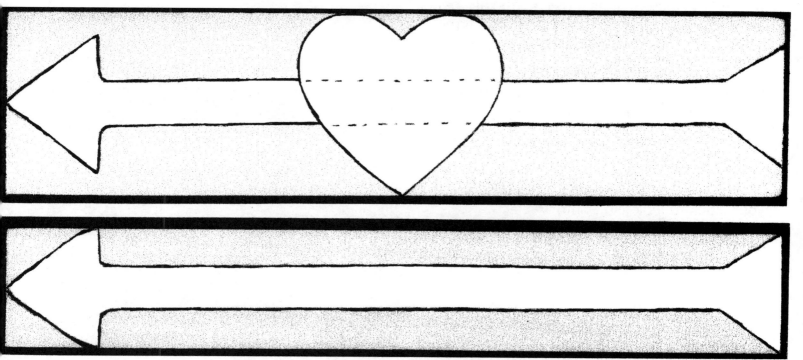

Photo #1: Traceable pattern for the Arrow Through the Heart

The Arrow Through the Heart is done in a 2-inch wide by 1¼-inch thick piece of bass wood 8¼ inches long. Using tracing paper, trace the pattern of Photo #1. Tape it firmly in place on the 2-inch wide side of your block.

Use an awl or a sharp, pointed knife and punch holes through the paper along the lines at ⅛-inch intervals about 1/16-inch deep.

Remove the paper and connect the dots with a pencil.

If you have a band saw or scroll saw, saw your block to look like Photo #2.

TIP: Unless you are very good with a saw, I

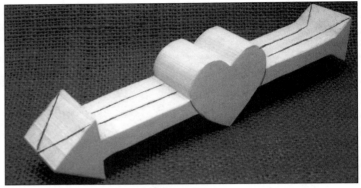

Photo #2

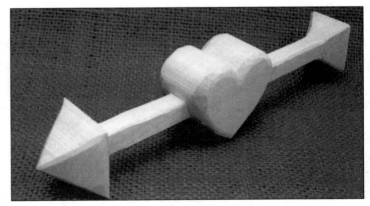

Photo #3

would recommend whittling your arrow through the heart from Photo #2 to look like Photo #4 or #5.

I used a saw, and believe me, I almost ruined the whole thing.

Note the saw mark on Photo #5.

When I got the piece looking like Photo #4, I thought, duh, this looks like a nail on the far end and a mushroom on the tip.

But, it didn't take long to make it look like an arrow …

Whoever saw a round arrowhead???

Photo #4

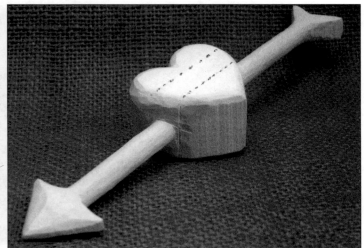

Photo #5

Whittling your arrow round is important, but getting it lined up so it goes through the heart very straight is the important step in this project.

It is not hard, but it is time-consuming.

Look and sight it from all directions, making sure it appears to go straight through. The dotted line will help.

In Photo #7, I have put a long dental pick in a wooden handle. The lower tool is a $3/16$-inch jig saw blade epoxied in a wooden handle. It curves up $1/2$ inch, so we

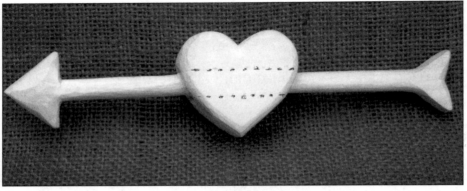

Photo #6

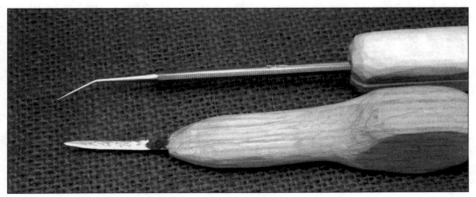

Photo #7

can push into the wood grain straight as in Photo #9.

The jig saw blade will bend a little without breaking. A knife blade, on the other hand, would break if we tried to bend it.

Note the shape of the blade. It is sharp on both sides and comes to a long, sweeping point.

It will enter the wood easily, not used as a saw but only to separate the fibers.

It is a long way through the way we are doing it.

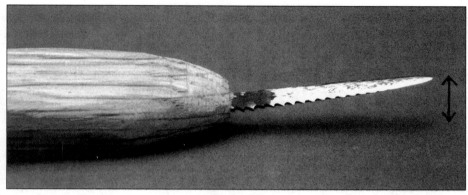

Photo #8

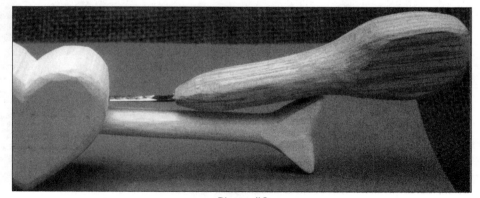

Photo #9

All the old-time whittlers went through the arrow the easy way. But I was never one to follow the crowd, so to speak. And, it seems I end up doing things the hard way.

The sharp, pointed knife and the small gouge can be used for the first ⅜ inch, but after that we will have to use our invented tools on this long journey through the heart.

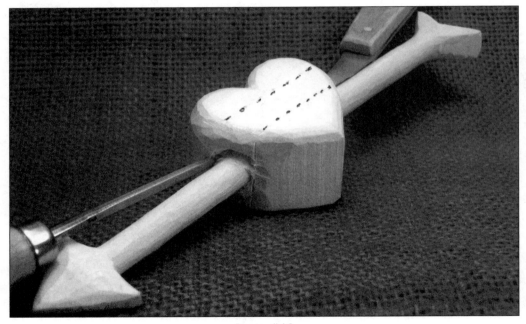

Photo #10

To tell the truth, I didn't know if this could be done when I started it. But I thought, boy, this would sure look neat if it could be done.

And it would sure as the world separate the men from the boys when it comes to whittling.

We will start the hole on both sides, making it about ⅛-inch larger than the arrow, and try to go through without cutting into the shaft.

When you get the hole in from both sides using the gouge and the knife, you should be in about ⅜ of an inch, as the photo shows here.

This will be as far as you can go with the gouge without damaging the shaft.

The dental pick with the long, curved point shown in Photo #7 can now be used to penetrate the wood, breaking the fibers of the wood about ⅟₁₆ to ⅛-inch around the shaft. This will tear and weaken the wood fibers.

Use the dental pick going around and around until it will go into the wood as if termites have eaten the wood into a mush.

Photo #11

Photo #12 shows how far into the wood the dental pick will go by taking advantage of the large hole we made with the gouge.

As you soften the wood with the dental pick on both sides, you can begin trying the jigsaw blade to see how far it will go.

As I tell you in the Ball in a Ball that Turns in a Cage, we are not trying to make chips, but only fine saw dust.

This will take two or three evenings to wear your way through the heart.

Photo #13 shows how far the blade will reach.

Photo #12

Photo #13

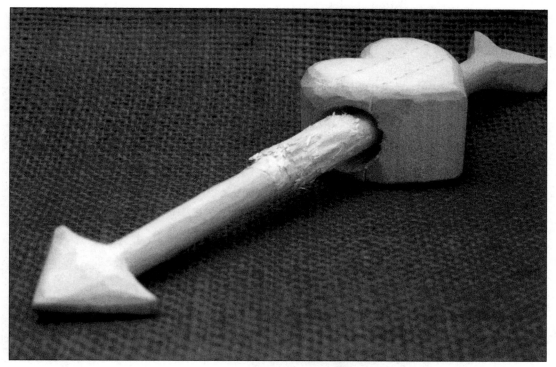

Photo #14

It's free at last, free like a bird from a cage. And the shaft is in good shape. All it needs now is an hour or so of whittling to take off the rough fibers, and a bit of clean-up work on the heart.

The Finished Arrow Through the Heart

And just think I had some doubt if it could be done. Sometimes failure is because we don't try.

The Cowboy Boot

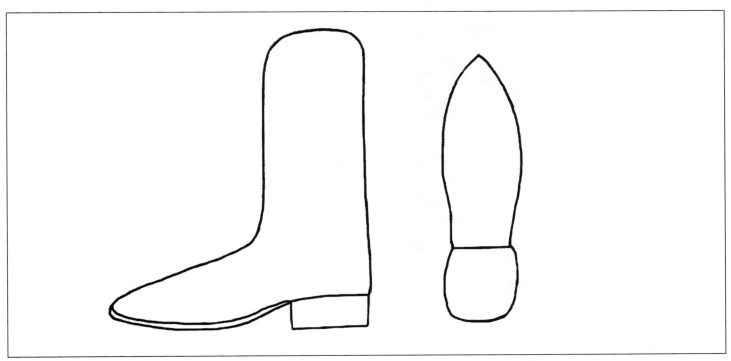

Photo #1: Traceable pattern for the cowboy boot

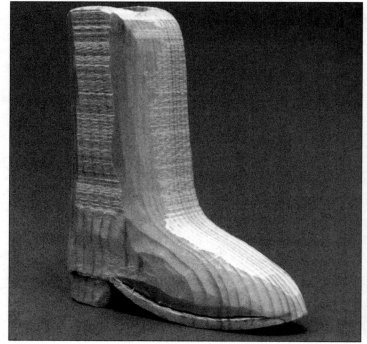

Photo #2

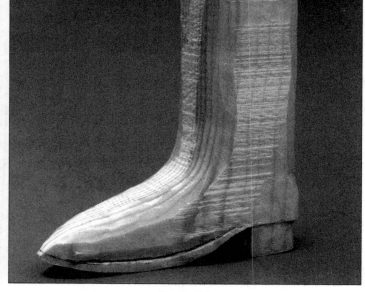

Photo #3

The cowboy boot is first sawed to size from the pattern. I like a change in wood every now and then. The boot is done in yellow pine here. I have sawed the shape and started whittling

The Finished Boot

the rough sawed piece to look as we see it here.

The smell of pine wood every now and then is a refreshing change from bass wood. Plus, you have to be on your toes to whittle pine. Because of the grain, it will split on you in a New York minute.

Tell your friends, "No, it's not ostrich skin, the anteater of calf skin, it's genuine PINE SKIN."

Look at the beautiful grain of the wood.

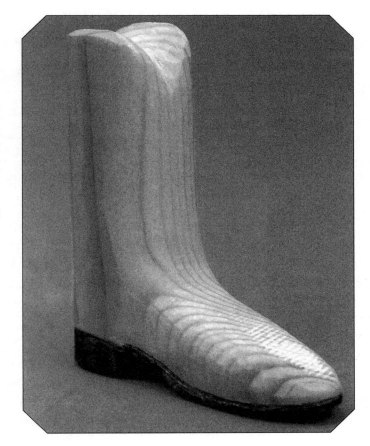

The L♥ve Sp♥♥ns

Photo #1

The Love Spoons are whittled from a 1-inch square by 18-inch long piece of bass wood. Photo #1 is the actual size. Use tracing paper and trace the spoon to the dotted line. We will need this pattern when we saw or whittle away the wood shown in Photo #2.

Love Spoon carving dates back to the mid 1600s. It is thought to have started when boys competing for a girl's love would whittle out a Love Spoon to try and beat out all the competi-tion. If the girl accepted the spoon, this meant she thought enough of the young man to be courted by him.

If the couple were married, the young man would then whittle two spoons connected by a chain.

Our Love Spoons will be joined by a wooden chain and will signify that a true and lasting love between two people is now bound together with a chain.

I will use a saw to remove both layers of wood shown here. If you do not have a saw, just whittle the wood away, but save your pattern of the spoon.

In Photo #3, I have sawed away the two pieces, leaving the ⅜-inch and ½-inch wood which will be the spoon and the handle.

Then using the pattern, I have traced the spoon drawing back on the cut away part.

In Photo #4, I have scooped out the spoon and started whittling.

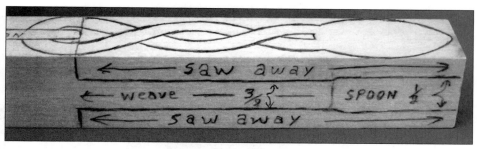

Photo #2

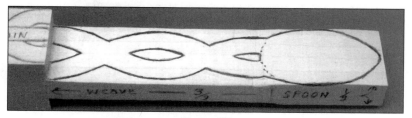

Photo #3

Photo #4

Scooping out the spoon can only be carved so deep with a straight-gouge or knife.

But the old-time whittlers figured out a way. They would scrape with a round-pointed knife or grind with a piece of sandstone, etc.

With the rough shape of the spoon and handle done, let's focus on joining the chain to the spoon. The unfinished spoon will be a lot easier to hold while we work on the chain.

In Photo #5, make a straight-in cut on each line ⅛-inch deep. The lines are ¼-inch apart. Now, whittle away the wood on each side of the chain bar to the depth of the spoon handle as shown in Photo #6.

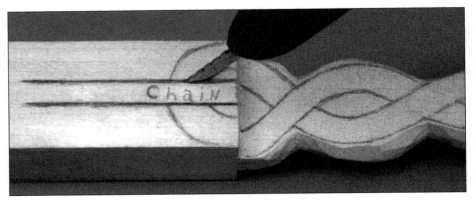
Photo #5

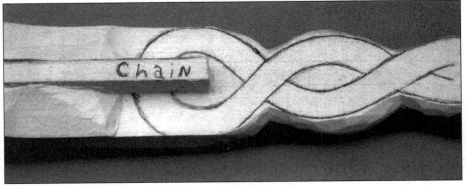
Photo #6

In Photo #7, I have turned the spoon to the opposite side and whittled it to be just like in Photo #6.

Now, trace the shape of the spoon on this side, and we will start whittling.

In Photo #8, I have whittled the chain bars to shape, and drawn in two more chain links.

Where the two little arrows are pointing, I have started a rounding cut. This will make the inside cut round like the outside cut, where the double-pointed arrow is.

In Photo #9, from the solid line (where the arrows point) to the dotted line will be the rounded edge. This rounded portion of the spoon handle will pass through the chain link.

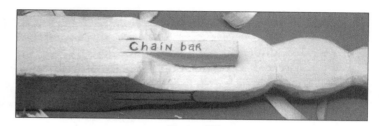

Photo #7

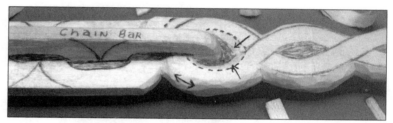

Photo #8

Photo #9

A side view here shows the rounded edge outlined in black (Photo #10).

All of the shaded area can now be carefully removed in the chain link and the spoon handle. Start by rounding the edge as shown in Photo #9.

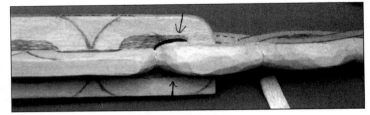

Photo #10

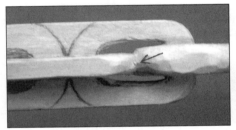

Photo #11

Photo #12

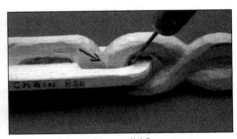

Photo #13

From Photo #10 to Photo #11, I have whittled through the chain. Photo #12 is whittled through the spoon.

I have left the wood where the arrows are pointing for strength while I make cut #13.

Use a hobby drill and a small, thin blade to make this cut.

In Photo #14, the cut to free the spoon is complete and the spoon is roughed out.

To get the spoon from rough-out to finished, expect to spend two or three evenings—the weave of the spoon is very time-consuming.

At this point, I like to whittle about four links free, then work on the other spoon until it's done.

On an 18-inch long piece of wood, you can expect to have at least 12 links of chain—more if you choose to make the links smaller.

About 40 hours on the Love Spoons so far … and counting.

Photo #14

Photo #15

The finished Love Spoons have 10 normal-sized links and 2 long links.

On one long link I have left enough wood for a heart and the words: Love is forever. On the backside, you can put the date, etc.

When whittling the chain from one spoon to the other, you can measure precisely and have all the links the same length—your choice.

Personally, I like to leave a space for a special message.

You can also whittle out the heart, leaving a hole to hang the spoons on a nail.

Expect to spend over a hundred hours on the spoons.

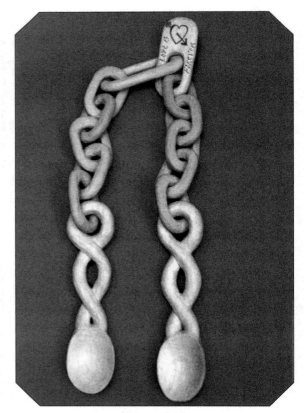

Photo #16

Tools for the Ball in a Spiral Cage on a Pedestal

There are very few tools I buy that I do not modify. With a rotary blade I ground the knife blade to this shape, to whittle the ball in the cage.

The rounded point is the only sharp edge on the blade. This helps protect the bars from being cut.

The gouge is a #7 by ³⁄₁₆. I also use a #3 by ⅛.

The screwdriver knife is a ³⁄₁₆-inch screwdriver inserted into a gouge-like handle, then sharpened on the point. It is used to make the straight-in cuts as I am doing in Photo #5.

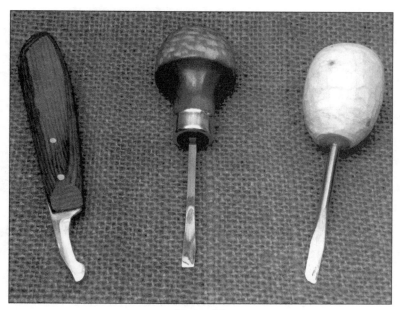

Photo #1

When grinding on tools, wear safety glasses—and keep the blade cool with water. If you get the blade hot, it will ruin the temper.

A Ball in a Spiral Cage on a Pedestal

To a non-whittler, a ball in a square cage or a round spiral cage would in all likelihood seem to be on the same skill level.

Most old-time whittlers can whittle a ball in a square cage without working up a sweat in the brain department.

But, a little more thought goes into the spiral cage. I use a piece of bass wood four inches long, by one and one-half inch square.

I like to make the spiral cage into what I call a "sitter," one that sits on its end on a shelf or on the mantle.

Leave a square end about ¾ inch long, and whittle the rest round as shown here in Photo #2.

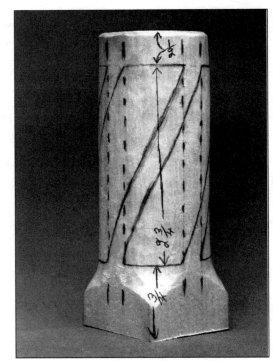

Photo #2

Laying out the bars for the cage is the most crucial step of the project. The cage bars are ¼-inch wide and about ¾-inch between bars.

The graph illustrates how the bars are drawn on the round block. Line 1 and 2 angle down ¼ turn to 1 and 2 on the bottom. The other three are drawn the same way.

In Photo #2, note the little lines below and above each bar. These are the lines to center the bars on the block. Put them on the square block before whittling it round. Then when whittling the block round on top, leave just enough of the pencil mark so you can remark it.

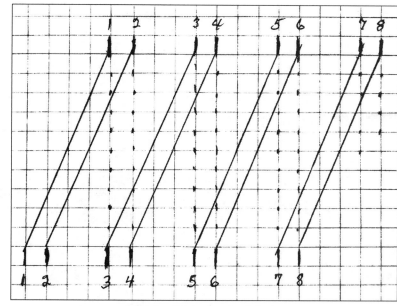

Photo #3 (not actual size)

Also, note the measurements shown on Photo #2—¾-inch from the bottom to the cage. The cage is 2¾ inches long. Leave a good ½ inch on top for strength.

Your block is now ready to expose the ball hidden inside.

In Photo #4, I have all the lines drawn in and ready for the screwdriver knife (note the arrows). Do not cut where the arrows are pointing, to do so would ruin the project.

The rounded shape of this piece makes it hard to hold, and a potential hazard to the hand. Use a non-slip surface and a safety glove. I like to use a pieced of burlap or leather tacked to my work bench.

Hold the screwdriver knife in your palm, with your fingers close to the point while making the straight-in cuts.

Cut all your lines about $\frac{3}{16}$-inch deep.

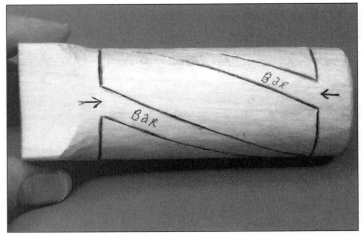

Photo #4

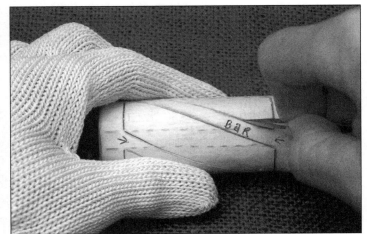

Photo #5

With all your lines cut ³⁄₁₆-inch deep, we are ready for the part I like best—sitting in my Lazy-Boy with a towel in my lap, a log on the fire, a sharp knife and a gouge.

Now, whittling friend, the time just seems to stand still. I hope I don't get involved and forget to take the next picture in the right sequence.

Believe me, in Book 1 I whittled right past where I should have taken a picture, then had to whittle the whole thing all over again to get the right picture.

Now, I take a photo every 10 minutes whether I need one or not, so I have a lot of photos I don't use.

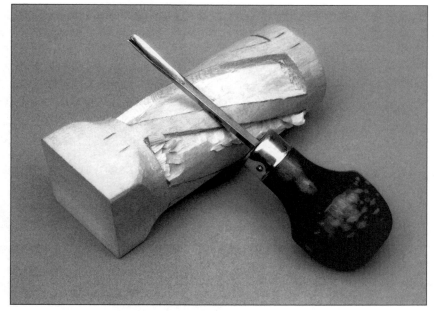

Photo #6

In Photo #6, I have one of the four sections gouged out ³⁄₁₆-inch deep and have started on the second section.

Let's get all four sections looking like the first one, then we will be ready for the next step.

Photo #7

With all four sections, one carved ³⁄₁₆ of an inch deep and looking like this one here in Photo #7, we are ready to start shaping the ball inside the base. The line around the inside sections is ½-inch from the top as the arrow shows.

This is where we will start rounding the ball inside the bars. Keep in mind the spiral bars are not as strong as square cage bars. This is because the spiral bars run across the grain.

For this reason, we will have to take some care to avoid breaking our masterpiece.

Leaving the ball attached to the block (where the circle is in Photo #8) will help strengthen the whimsie while doing the heavy whittling.

Now, draw a line around the inside section 1¼ inch from the top as shown here, in Photo #8.

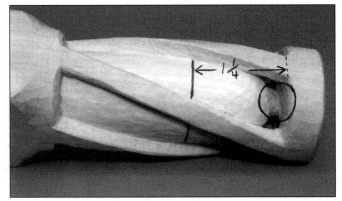

Photo #8

In Photo #9, I have drawn little ⅛-inch arrows pointing to the line. Now, make a straight-in cut about ⅛-inch deep on the line around the block. On this cut you can use the screwdriver knife or a round, pointed knife, but this is a dangerous cut so be sure to wear your safety glove.

In Photo #10, with my ³⁄₁₆, 5 gouge, I have started at the tail of the arrows, cutting toward the straight-in cut.

Work your way around the line on the block to the depth of the straight-in cut.

Now, make the straight-in cut a little deeper and gouge around another time or two. Be very careful not to damage the bars.

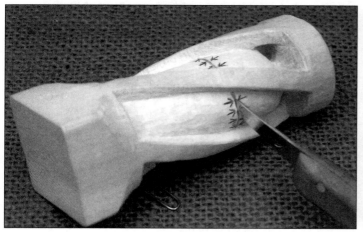

Photo #9

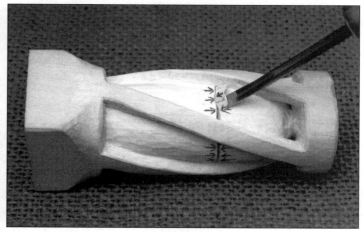

Photo #10

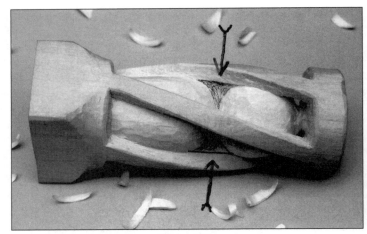

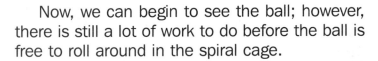

Photo #11

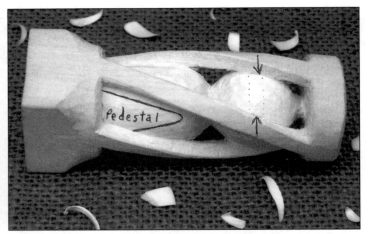

Photo #12

Now, we can begin to see the ball; however, there is still a lot of work to do before the ball is free to roll around in the spiral cage.

With the gouge and knife we can now begin removing the wood where the arrows are pointing (the shaded area). In Photo #11, whittling friends, we are now down to the nitty-gritty.

I have drawn in the pedestal and put two arrows pointing to where the ball should be left attached to all four bars as long as possible while whittling the ball smaller and smaller.

We can also start removing some wood from around the pedestal. From here on it is TINY CHIPS and lots of PATIENCE!

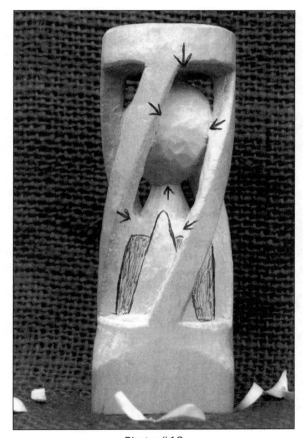

Photo #13

Photo #13 is shown in actual size, so we can see what we have done and where we are going.

The ball is a bit smaller, but still attached where the arrows are pointing.

The pedestal has started to take shape. The next step will be to remove the shaded area around the pedestal, but leave it attached to the ball and the bars where the arrows are.

The spiral cage bars are for the most part square in shape where the square cage bars are triangular in shape. This means the ball in our spiral cage here will be smaller than its cousin in the square cage.

We are beginning to sweat in the brain department, I think.

Let's whittle …

From Photo #13 to Photo #14, I have whittled the ball small enough to free it from the bars but left it attached on top and to the pedestal.

The pedestal is still attached to the ball and the four bars, so let's whittle it to the size shown here, but leave it attached to the bars where the arrows are.

Now, we will free the ball from the pedestal and the top of the cage and whittle it as round as possible before freeing the pedestal from the bars.

Work gently, now, so as not to break the fragile spiral bars.

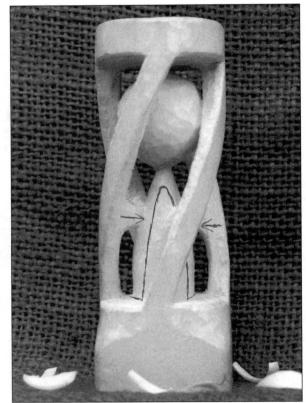

Photo #14

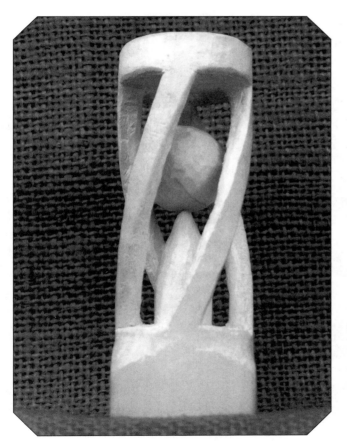

Ball in Spiral Cage on a Pedestal

Like a king on his throne, our ball sits proudly on its own pedestal in a spiral cage.

I suppose there have been old-timers who have whittled balls in spiral cages, but so far I have not been able to find a photo of one.

If a friend should ask how you got the ball in a spiral cage, sitting on a pedestal, just say, "Oh, they grow that way if the chips fall the right way!"

Ball in a Ball That Turns in a Cage

The old timers whittled balls in balls, but the round cages were very fragile and had to be handled like an egg.

When I began thinking about projects to put in Book 2, the ball in a ball was not on the list until the thought hit me: Why not put the balls in a cage? Not in just any cage, but a cage in which the balls couldn't touch the bars. Suspend the balls on a rod attached to the sides or ends of the larger cage! But, how?

Then, my whittling friend, the Lollipop Behind Bars in Book 1 popped into my head.

That's it! Make a Lollipop with two sticks, but in a 2 x 2 bass wood block.

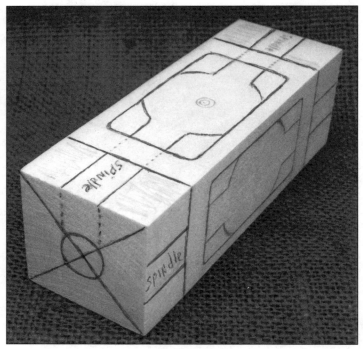

Photo #1

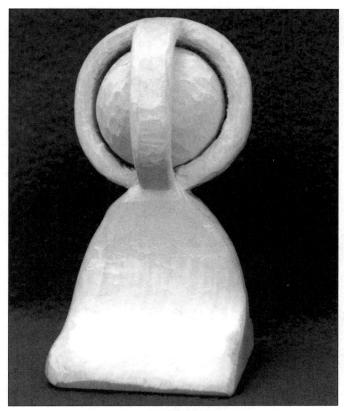

Photo #2

The 2 x 2 block is six inches long. The ball on the spindle will be almost 1⅞ inches in diameter.

To find the center on the ends of the block, draw a straight line from corner to corner. Where the lines cross will be the center of the spindle as you see in Photo #1.

The spindle will be about ⅝ inch in diameter, a bit smaller won't hurt because this project is big enough—1/16 of an inch will not destroy it. However, the spindle should be whittled round and straight.

In Book 1 I show a photo in the back of the book of things to do until we whittle together again. The Ball in a Ball on a Pedestal was one of those things. The reason I put it on a pedestal was so it wouldn't get broken so easily.

Our Ball in a Ball that Turns in a Cage will be whittled to look like the ball shown here.

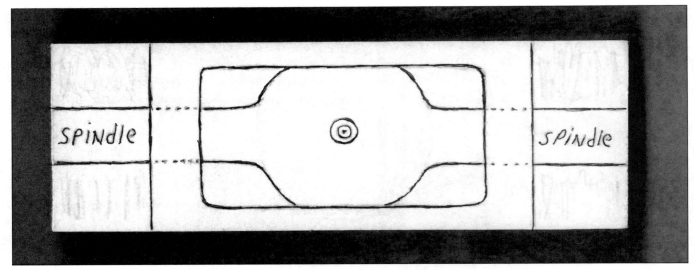

Photo #3

This is the actual size pattern for all four sides of your 2 x 2 x 6-inch block of bass wood.

Trace four patterns and tape them tightly to your block where it will not slip.

With the patterns taped firmly in place, use an awl or sharp, pointed knife and punch holes along the lines 1/8-inch apart, making them about 1/16 inch deep in the wood.

Take the paper off and connect the dots. All four sides will be done alike.

With all four sides drawn in, we can make the straight-in cuts ⅛-inch deep. The corners of the cage being round, a small, sharp, pointed knife blade will do a better job. The screwdriver knife does a good job on the long cuts.

Photo #4

If you didn't make a screwdriver knife, a skew can be bought at woodcarving stores (town-bought screwdriver knife).

I didn't draw the ball and spindle on the top side in Photo #4. The lines showing on top of Photo #4 will be the only lines we make the straight-down cuts, on all four sides. These kinds of cuts should be made on a non-slip surface with a safety glove on the hand holding the work piece.

Make the straight-down or straight-in cuts on all four sides on the lines shown here on the top side of Photo #4.

Now we are ready to start removing some wood. Drawing lines is boring for me!

All the straight-in cuts were done in Photo #4.

Now all there is to do is remove wood on all four sides as we have started doing here in Photo #5.

I am using a #5 curve ³⁄₁₆-inch gouge.

After some three more hours of whittling, our masterpiece should look like Photo #6.

Don't get too involved in whittling and whittle the spindle too little.

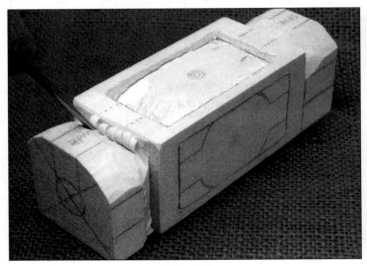

Photo #5

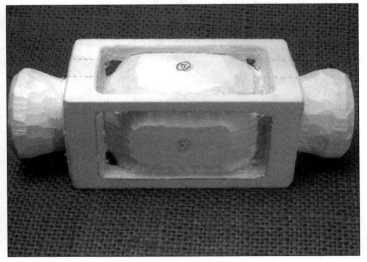

Photo #6

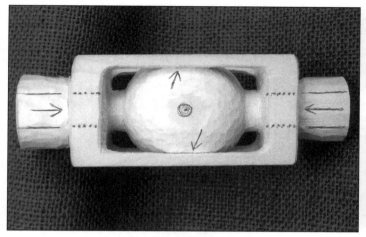

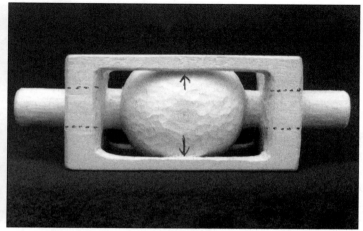

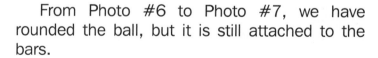

Photo #7

Photo #8

From Photo #6 to Photo #7, we have rounded the ball, but it is still attached to the bars.

The dotted lines on the cage show where the spindle will pass through and turn in the cage.

Now, let's whittle the spindle down to the size of the lines drawn on them.

The spindles now appear to go straight through where the dotted lines are on the cage.

Do not cut the spindles through the cage. And leave the ball attached to the cage bars where the arrows are pointing. This will give the project strength while we whittle the ball inside the ball.

Photo #9

Laying out the cage on the round ball, I use a small screwdriver knife to make an indentation, marking the low point of the cage.

The tool making the straight-in cuts should always be pointing to the center of the ball as shown here by the arrow.

Mark all the low points on the ball.

The bars will be straight under the square cage bars ³⁄₈-inch wide. Then curve to the low point you made with the screwdriver knife.

When the four sides of the cage are drawn, we are ready for the straight-in cuts.

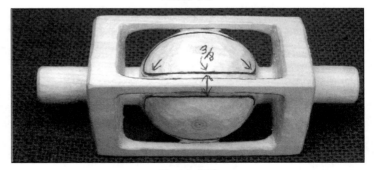

Photo #10

It's time to start the straight-in cuts on the ball in the square cage.

Note, I am wearing the safety glove, and the cage is sitting on its edge. As I mentioned, all the straight-in cuts need to be made toward the center of the ball.

I use a small screwdriver knife to make these delicate cuts. A ⅛-inch screwdriver with the point sharpened and rounded, and a wooden handle fitted over the plastic handle makes a better tool for these cuts than you can buy anywhere.

Wear the safety glove and hold the work piece securely, making the cuts carefully and only ⅛-inch deep.

Do not use force. Instead, gently rock the tool back and forth. We have too much time invested in our whimsie to break it now.

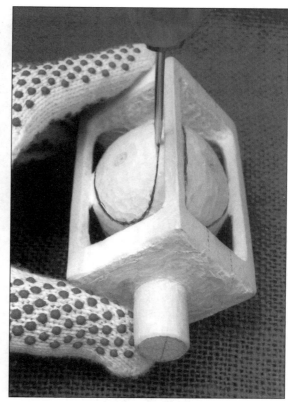

Photo #11

Photo #12

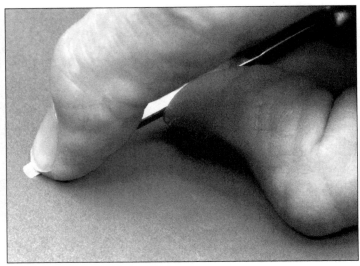

Photo #13

Carefully, with the gouge and the ball whittling knife, I have started the cut. Use the knife where the pencil is pointing, and the gouge where the arrow is pointing. The small gouge seems to work better on the ends. But the wood on the ends will split very easily, so hold the gouge in such a way that it cannot go but ⅛-inch deep, as shown in Photo #13.

When you get all the way around the straight-in cut, you will have to deepen the cut ⅛-inch deeper, where the pencil is pointing. The wood in the middle where the oval circles are can be removed with the knife or the ³⁄₁₆-inch gouge.

Photo #14

Photo #15

Where the arrow is should be ¼ inch. I have removed most of the wood where the oval circles were. We need to smooth the inner ball until it is as round as you can get it. All four sides will be done the same way.

You can now see why we left the ball and spindles attached.

Our inner ball is now round as a full moon in June and almost as pretty. All the round cage bars should now be ¼-inch thick and ⅜-inch wide. Now is where the fun begins. We will have to whittle the inner ball ¹/₁₆-inch smaller, and undercut the bars to free our pretty ball.

(Another week? Maybe not.)

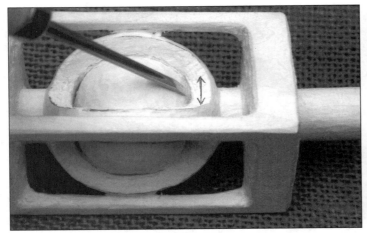

Photo #16

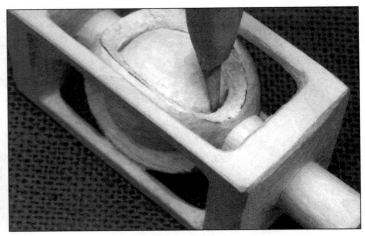

Photo #17

We will start our undercuts at the most difficult place. I like to get the hard part first. I use the small gouge, not as a gouge, but more like a saw or scraper. Rubbing the gouge back and forth, as the arrows show, will slowly make sawdust. Turn the gouge over, curve side up, then curve side down. Keep in mind the ball still needs to be round.

The gouge will get you about ¼-inch deep. The dental pick and the sharp, pointed knife can be used when the gouge has reached its depth.

We are not trying to remove chips here, only sawdust. Use the knife and the dental pick like the gouge, back and forth.

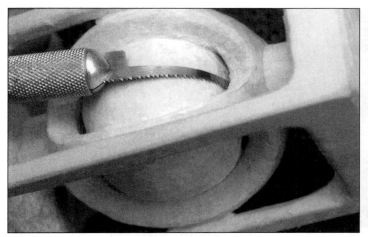

Photo #18

Photo #19

It took about three hours per end with the gouge, knife and dental pick to make the cut here where the saw blade is.

Tip: The cut I made around the ball is round, therefore, I could not see through the cut, so I put a bend in the saw blade and worked it over the ball. When the saw blade would go around all eight sides, I knew the cut was complete.

Now it is time to free the inner ball.

With the sharp, pointed knife, start making ⅛-inch deep undercuts under both sides of the four round cages. Work gently until these cuts are made.

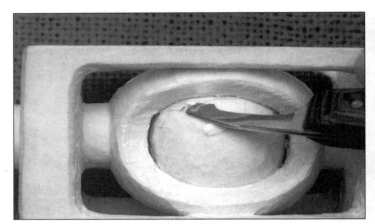

Photo #20

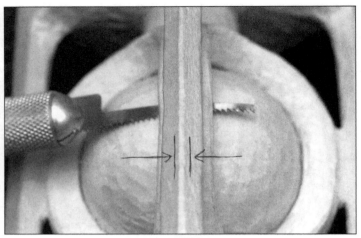

Photo #21

When you have the $\frac{1}{16}$-inch deep undercuts made with the sharp, pointed knife, start shaving the ball slightly smaller with the ball-whittling knife.

Whittle under each bar as deep as the undercut made with the sharp, pointed knife. This will give us room to scrape the rest of the way under the bar.

When you have about one half of the undercut made from each side, as the arrows pointing to the lines show, you can work the sharp, pointed knife through.

Then take the knife out and work the saw blade through where the knife was. Then gently saw the remainder of the undercut.

Photo #22

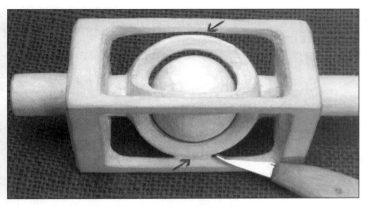

Photo #23

When you saw away the remaining fibers, the ball will not turn very well until you do a lot more whittling and shaving with the ball-whittling knife.

I like to shade the high spots on the ball with a pencil, then whittle them off.

Turn the ball, shade the high spots and whittle; turn, shade, whittle. It took me two evenings, six hours total, to get the ball pretty and round.

It's time to free the big ball from the bars.

This is a simple whittling job after rounding the ball. On the top bar I have shaved away the wood between the round cage and the square cage.

Now, let's whittle the other three like the one on top.

Well, at last we are ready to do the old whittle-around-the-spindle trick.

This is not as hard as it may seem, especially if you did the Lollipop Behind the Bars in Book 1.

Since Book 1, I have adopted the hook-bill knife for this kind of cut. Some carvers call this kind of knife an eye knife.

The hook-bill knife will go into the wood as shown here, ⅜-inch deep. Make the cut flat against the spindle all the way around it.

Work it in as far is it will go, several times around. Any thin, sharp blade can be used. I just like the hook-bill.

Photo #24

Then, as shown, use the small gouge to remove the wood at the angle shown. *But,* do not cut into the spindle. The knife will go in a little deeper after you use the gouge.

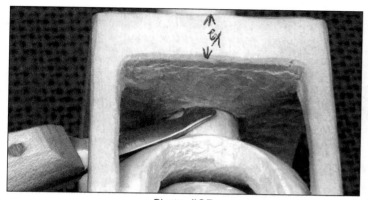

Photo #25

Photo #26

The ball-whittling knife works well on the inside. It will cut in a little over ⅛-inch deep. Then use the small gouge like the angle cut we made on the outside.

When you get the gouge cut made, the knife will go in a bit deeper. Now you should be almost through the ½-inch wall of the cage. But, there will still be fibers holding the spindle to the cage.

Now, with a long, thin blade gently work it in through the remaining fibers. Be very careful, do not get your hand in the way if the knife slips.

Put a mark on the knife blade so you will know when the knife should make its way through the wood.

Photo #27

If you go in at the wrong angle, the blade will go into the spindle or the cage. So sight it up and go easy.

The knife blade going through wood was only to make an opening for the saw blade.

As you can see here in Photo #27, the saw blade has a slight bend. This will keep the point of the saw blade from gouging into the spindle.

Saw gently, taking your time, making sure the cut is being made close to the spindle and not cutting into the cage wall.

When you get this end of the spindle free, all you lack then will be the spindle on the other end.

Do it just like we did this end, and the balls will be ready to show and tell.

Ball in a Ball that Turns in a Cage

The cage bars on the big ball are larger than the bars of the square cage.

This is because the distance is greater from corner to corner.

Jack is sitting on the front porch of the house his great-grandfather built in northwest Jack County, Texas, in 1877. Jack's grandfather, 17 at the time, and his two brothers helped build this pioneer house. Jack's cousin, Jim, and his wife have restored the house without changing its original looks and now make it their home.

The four-foot long, split-chain Jack is holding is attached to a Heart in a Heart all whittled from one piece of wood.